Key Publication Project for the 13th Five-Year Plan of China
Sponsored by the State Ethnic Affairs Commission
and the "985 Project (2nd phase)" of Lanzhou University

"十三五"国家重点出版物出版规划项目
国家民委资助项目
兰州大学"985 工程"二期资助项目

Illustrated Introductions to Ethnic Minorities in China

中国少数民族图志

(NORTHWEST VOLUME)
（西北卷）

Editor-in-chief: Yang Jianxin
Executive Editor-in-chief: Zhao Lisheng
Written by Zhao Xuan and Yang Linkun
Translated by Zhao Xuan

主　编／杨建新
执行主编／赵利生
编　著／赵　璇　杨林坤
英文翻译／赵　璇

THE ETHNIC PUBLISHING HOUSE
民族出版社

The Tatar Ethnic Group

塔塔尔族

图书在版编目(CIP)数据

塔塔尔族：英汉对照 / 赵璇，杨林坤编著. -- 北京：民族出版社，2023.10
（中国少数民族图志 / 杨建新主编. 西北卷）
ISBN 978-7-105-17113-2

Ⅰ.①塔… Ⅱ.①赵… ②杨… Ⅲ.①塔塔尔族 - 民族志 - 中国 - 图集 Ⅳ.①K284.2-64

中国国家版本馆CIP数据核字（2023）第207942号

中国少数民族图志（西北卷）·塔塔尔族（英汉对照）

丛书策划	杨青	
责任编辑	赵莹	
装帧设计	金晔	
出版发行	民族出版社	
地　　址	北京市和平里北街14号	
邮　　编	100013	
网　　址	http://www.mzpub.com	
印　　刷	北京盛通印刷股份有限公司	
经　　销	各地新华书店	
版　　次	2023年11月第1版　　2023年11月北京第1次印刷	
开　　本	787毫米×1092毫米　　1/16	
字　　数	20千字	
印　　张	5	
定　　价	49.80元	
书　　号	ISBN 978-7-105-17113-2/K · 2938（汉1688）	

该书若有印装质量问题，请与本社发行部联系退换　发行部电话：010-64224782

编委会名单

主　　编　杨建新

执行主编　赵利生

编委（以姓氏笔画为序）

王　力	王希隆	王建新
王海飞	切　排	闫丽娟
李　洁	李　静	李有明
杨　青	杨文炯	杨林坤
武　沐	周传斌	宗喀·漾正冈布
赵利生	徐黎丽	高永久

The Compilation Committee

Editor-in-chief: Yang Jianxin
Executive Editor-in-chief: Zhao Lisheng

Members of the Committee (in alphabetic order)

Gao Yongjiu ◎ Li Jie ◎ Li Jing

Li Youming ◎ Qie Pai ◎ Wang Haifei

Wang Jianxin ◎ Wang Li ◎ Wang Xilong

Wu Mu ◎ Xu Lili ◎ Yan Lijuan

Yang Linkun ◎ Yang Qing ◎ Yang Wenjiong

Yongdrol K. Tsongkha ◎ Zhao Lisheng ◎ Zhou Chuanbin

Preface

We now present a series of illustrated introductions to ethnic minorities in China and its Northwest Volume has been a product of conscientious organization and writing of numerous teachers at Center for Studies of Ethnic Minorities in NorthWest China of Lanzhou University—a key humanities and social sciences research center with the Ministry of Education of China. Its accomplishment and publication commends my sincere congratulations and praise!

Center for Studies of Ethnic Minorities in NorthWest China of Lanzhou University is an advanced institute for teaching of and study on issues concerning ethnic groups in China. It trains master and doctoral candidates in ethnology and hosts a post-doctoral research station too. Each year two scores or so higher-level students majoring in ethnology are being trained here and quite a number of monographs and hundreds of papers are being written and published by them and their supervisors. Some may ask, is it worthwhile for such a high-level research institute to invest so much manpower and fund into such a series of popular readings? My answer is a definite "yes"!

It is quite natural for an advanced research institute and its members to come up with higher-level, big-volumed, high-quality and front-lined academic works, but it is also very recommendable for them to produce for non-professionals and general readers profound-in-idea but easy-to-understand and interesting popular materials, for enhancing the cultural literacy of people.

China is a country with multiple ethnic groups and the Chinese history has been created and developed by all of them. The revival of the Great Chinese Dream requires the concerted efforts of all the peoples in China. Every ethnic group in China boasts its own long-established and colorful culture and, dwelling in its respective beautiful habitat, has been a master of its own and also of the whole country, constituting a basic force in constructing this great socialist country of ours with strong Chinese characteristics. All the peoples in China should respect and help each other and work together to foster a prosperous country. Keeping this basic national situation in mind and actively participating into the great cause of strengthening our national unity will doubtlessly ensure the successful implementation of the various ethnic policies formulated by the Communist Party of China and lay a solid foundation for ethnic harmony, frontier security and national unity. This long-term endeavor needs step-by-step efforts and gradual understanding of all the peoples. In my opinion, writing such a popular series on the ethnic histories and cultures of China for all within and outside of this country constitutes one of the meaningful projects for the ultimate purpose of uniting all ethnic groups of our great nation!

I believe this series of illustrated introductions will certainly serve this purpose!

September, 2014
Yang Jianxin

序

　　这部图志是普及我国民族知识的科普读物。经过教育部人文社会科学重点研究基地——兰州大学西北少数民族研究中心精心组织和多名老师的辛勤劳动，终于完成了西北卷的编写任务，我觉得值得庆贺与赞扬。

　　兰州大学西北少数民族研究中心，是我国研究民族问题的高级科研教学机构，培养民族学硕士、博士并设有博士后科研流动站，每年培养四五十位民族学高级人才、有数部专著和近百篇优秀论文问世。这样一个高级科研单位，投入较大的人力、资金编写这样一套科普读物值不值得？在一些人的脑海中是有疑问的。而我认为，这很有必要、非常值得。

　　高级研究机构和高级研究人员，推出高、大、精、专、尖、新的研究成果是理所当然的，而为非专业人员和广大老百姓创作出深入浅出、引人入胜的科普读物，提升直接服务社会的能力，则是应该大力提倡的。

　　中国是多民族的国家，中国的历史，是中国各民族共同书写的，中华民族伟大复兴的中国梦，要靠各民族共同奋斗才能实现。各民族都有自己悠久的历史、灿烂的文化、美丽的家园，都是国家的主人，都是建设中国特色社会主义伟大强国的基本力量，应该相互尊重、相互帮助、共同团结奋斗、共同繁荣发展。只有广大老百姓认识到这个道理，认识到中国的这个基本国情，并积极主动投入到民族团结进步的伟大事业中，中国共产党制定的各项民族政策，才能真正落到实处，才能为我国的民族团结、边疆稳定、国家统一奠定深厚的群众基础。这个基础是需要一点一滴积累、需要长期坚持宣传教育、需要在广大老百姓的心里构建的。我认为，面对广大普通老百姓和国内外一切需要了解我国少数民族情况的人群，提供这样一部科普读物，就是打造和构建这个基础的一项工作。

　　期待图志能起到这种作用。

杨建新

2014 年 10 月

目　录 Contents

　　塔塔尔族 是中国 56 个民族之一，中华民族大家庭的一员。"塔塔尔"，是塔塔尔语 "tatar" 的汉语翻译名词。唐代汉文文献称其为"达旦"，之后文献里出现的"达达""达怛""达靼""鞑靼"等，都是"塔塔尔"的不同音译。中华人民共和国成立后，依照本民族广大群众的意愿，"塔塔尔"一词正式成为中文书写的族别称谓。

The Tatar people is one of the 56 recognized ethnicities in China and is an integral part of the Chinese national family. The term "Tatar" is the Chinese translation of the word "tatar" from the Tatar language. In Chinese literature from the Tang dynasty, they were referred to as "Dadan" (达旦). Subsequent documents feature terms like "Dada" (达达), "Dadan" (达怛), "Datan" (达靼), and "Datang" (鞑靼), all of which are different phonetic translations of the term "Tatar". After the establishment of the People's Republic of China, in line with the wishes of the majority of the Tatar community, the term "Tatar" was formally designated as the Chinese ethnonym for this ethnic group.

自然风光 *Natural scenery*

文化石 Culture stone

　　塔塔尔族 人口共有 3544 人（2021 年），是我国人口较少的民族之一。塔塔尔族属于蒙古人种西伯利亚类型，生活在我国新疆地区，散居在天山北部地区，主要分布在伊犁哈萨克自治州、昌吉回族自治州、乌鲁木齐市等地区。其中，昌吉回族自治州奇台县大泉塔塔尔族乡是全国唯一的塔塔尔民族乡。

塔塔尔族男女青年 *Young men and women of the Tatar people*

The Tatar people,classified under the Siberian subtype of the Mongolian race, has a population of 3,544 (as of 2021), making them one of China's smaller ethnic groups. Predominantly residing in Xinjiang, they're spread across the northern regions of the Tianshan Mountains. Their main settlements are in the Kazakh Autonomous Prefecture of Ili, the Hui Autonomous Prefecture of Changji, and the city of Urumqi. Notably, Daquan Tatar People Township in Qitai County of the Hui Autonomous Prefecture of Changji stands as the sole Tatar people township in China.

美丽塔塔尔 *Beautiful Tatar*

塔塔尔族 是一个有着悠久历史的民族，它是由许多不同部落长期融合而成的，其中保加尔人（或称不里阿耳人）、钦察人和蒙古人是主要组成部分。

The Tatars possess a long and storied history, evolving from the union of numerous tribes over extended periods. Major tribal groups that formed the Tatar people include the Bulgars (also known as the Bulghar people), the Kipchaks, and the Mongols.

塔塔尔青年的雕塑
Sculpture of Tatar young people

　　13 世纪初,成吉思汗孙拔都在伏尔加河一带建立了横跨欧亚大陆的钦察汗国（也称金帐汗国）。保加尔人、钦察人和鞑靼人等均为其属民,之后统称为塔塔尔。15 世纪,金帐汗国趋于瓦解,在伏尔加河、卡马河流域,建立以保加尔人为主体的喀山汗国,他们与钦察人、鞑靼人和蒙古人相互融合,逐渐形成塔塔尔人。塔塔尔人从 19 世纪初陆续进入我国新疆地区。长期以来,塔塔尔族与汉族、维吾尔族、哈萨克族、乌孜别克族等各民族交往交流交融,其文化早已深深扎根于中华文明的沃土之中,成为中华民族的组成部分,与其他各民族一道诠释铸牢中华民族共同体的华美篇章。

塔塔尔族羊图腾雕塑
Sculpture of the Tatar sheep totem

In the early 13th century, Batu Khan, Genghis Khan's grandson, established the Kipchak Khanate (often referred to as the Golden Horde) that spanned the vast expanses of Europe and Asia near the Volga River. This khanate encompassed various tribes, including the Bulgars, Kipchaks, and Tatars. Subsequently, these tribes were collectively termed "Tatars". By the 15th century, as the Golden Horde began its decline, the Kazan Khanate arose in the regions surrounding the Volga and Kama rivers. Dominated mainly by the Bulgars, it witnessed the merging of the Kipchaks, Tatars, and Mongols, which led to the dis-

自然风光 *Natural scenery*

tinct formation of the Tatar people.

Starting from the early 19th century, the Tatars commenced their migration into the Xinjiang region of China. Over the decades, they've engaged in deep cultural exchanges and integration with other ethnicities, such as the Han, Uyghur, Kazakh, and Uzbek people. Their culture, enriched by these interactions, has taken root in the fertile grounds of Chinese civilization. The Tatars now stand as a vital component of the broader Chinese national mosaic, jointly contributing to the shared narrative and identity of the Chinese nation.

中国传统村落

魅力塔塔尔   美丽大泉湖

村大门 *Village gate*

自然风光 *Natural scenery*

中华人民共和国 成立后，塔塔尔人在社会的各行各业都为实现中国特色社会主义现代化而努力奋斗。昌吉州奇台县大泉塔塔尔族乡成立于 1989 年 7 月，是全国唯一的塔塔尔民族乡。

塔塔尔族青年男女
Young man and women of the Tatar people

Since the establishment of the People's Republic of China, the Tatars have worked tirelessly across diverse sectors in pursuit of socialist modernization imbued with Chinese characteristics. The Daquan Tatar People Township, situated in Qitai County of Changji Prefecture, was inaugurated in July 1989, marking it as the singular Tatar People Township throughout China.

大泉塔塔尔乡秋牧场 *Autumn pasture in Daquan Tatar People Township*

全乡　土地面积约 1400 平方千米，其中草场 162.4 万亩。大泉乡地势北低南高，大致分为南部天山牧业区和北部大泉湖农业区两部分。南部天山牧业区从东往西四条沟依次分布着 4 个牧业村，主要发展畜牧业；北部大泉湖农业区分布着 3 个农业村和 4 个牧业村的定居点，主要从事种植业生产，主要农作物有小麦、玉米、甜菜等。农家乐旅游等第三产业发展出现了热潮。

The entire township spans an area of approximately 1,400 square kilo-meters, inclusive of a grassland covering 1.624 million mu. The terrain is characterized by its lower elevations in the north and higher elevations in the south. Broadly, the township is segmented into two primary regions: the Mount Tianshan Pastoral Region in the south and the Daquan Lake Agricultural Area in the north. The Mount Tianshan Pastoral Region hous-es four pastoral villages, laid out from east to west, primarily dedicated

大泉塔塔尔乡政府 *Daquan Tatar People Township Government*

to livestock farming. Conversely, the Daquan Lake Agricultural Area in the north consists of three agricultural villages and settlement points for four pastoral villages, where the primary activity is crop farming. Predominant crops here include wheat, corn, and sugar beet. Additionally, the rise of tertiary industries, notably agritourism, has become a prominent trend in the township.

乡间小道 *Township rural path*

塔塔尔语 属阿尔泰语系突厥语族克普恰克语支，是在保加尔语和克普恰克语的基础上发展形成的。古回鹘语、喀卡尼亚语、古乌孜别克语都对它产生过影响。从 20 世纪中叶开始，塔塔尔族对原有的塔塔尔文进行了改革。现代塔塔尔文语音由 10 个元音单位、24 个辅音音位组成。

The Tatar language falls under the Qypchaq branch of the Turkic language family within the broader Altaic linguistic group. It has evolved primarily from the Bulgar and Qypchaq languages, with influences from the ancient Uyghur, Karakhanid, and old Uzbek languages. Starting from the mid-20th century, the Tatar people began reforming the original Tatar script. The phonetics of the modern Tatar language consist of 10 vowel sounds and 24 consonantal phonemes.

我国 塔塔尔族生活在一个多语言并存的环境下，多语兼用是其语言的特色。一般在民族内部交流时使用本民族语言，同时又兼用国家通用语、哈萨克语、维吾尔语等多种语言。

乡间道路 *Township road*

In China, the Tatar community thrives in a multilingual setting, making multilingualism a distinguishing characteristic of their linguistic behavior. While they typically converse in the Tatar language amongst themselves, they are also proficient in various languages, including the nation's official language, as well as Kazakh and Uyghur languages.

（一）教育 Education

根据 2021 年第七次全国人口普查数据，塔塔尔族人口为 3544 人，其中高级知识分子有 350 人，属于我国受教育程度较高的民族之一。

According to the data from the seventh national population census in 2021, the population of the Tatar people stands at 3,544, with 350 of them being highly educated intellectuals. This makes the Tatar one of the ethnic groups in China with a higher level of education.

幼儿园 Kindergarden

中心小学广场 *Central elementary school square*

　　大泉塔塔尔族乡 中心小学始建于 1984 年，是全国唯一一所塔塔尔民族小学。学校占地面积 3 万多平方米，现有 11 个教学班，在校生 319 名，教职工 56 人。学校中心位置是广场国旗杆，旗杆后有一幢两层教学楼。教室宽敞明亮，每间教室都配备了多媒体设备。学校走廊上张贴了学生以爱党爱国、各民族团结友爱为主题创作的绘画、摄影、诗歌、作文等作品。

The Central Primary School in Daquan Tatar People Township, established in 1984, is the only primary school in the country dedicated to the Tatar people. The school spans over 30,000 square meters and currently has 11 teaching classes, accommodating 319 students with a staff of 56. The focal point of the school is a square featuring the national flag pole, situated in front of a two-story academic building. Classrooms are spacious and well-lit, each equipped with multimedia devices. The school's corridors are adorned with student artwork, which centers on themes of patriotism, love for the party and nation, and unity and friendship among various ethnicities.

小学教室 *Elementary school classroom*

中心小学校门 *Gate of central primary school*

小学教学楼内
Inside the teaching building of elementary school

小学生手抄报
Elementary school transcript

小学文化墙
*Elementary school
cultural wall*

（二）医疗 Health care

　　大泉塔塔尔族乡　卫生院位于乡政府南侧 500 米左右，院内有一栋朝南两层高的白色拱顶建筑。该卫生院兼具门诊开药和住院治疗两大功能。大厅是一个不规则圆形区域，地面由红白两色砖块交错拼贴而成，墙面由淡蓝色和白色粉刷而成。大厅右侧是 B 超室和眼科门诊，左侧的通道里是其他科室的门诊。楼梯在大厅正中间，二楼是中医特色诊室和住院输液区。这所卫生院主要为大泉塔塔尔族乡居民提供日常医疗保健服务。

卫生院门 *Township hospital gate*

体检室 *Physical examination room*

卫生院 *Township hospital*

卫生院内的中医馆
*Traditional Chinese Medicine Hall
in the Township hospital*

卫生院大厅
Township hospital hall

The Daquan Tatar People Township Health Center is positioned approximately 500 meters south of the township government. Within its premises stands a white, two-story building with a characteristic arch-shaped roof. This health center functions both as an outpatient prescription service and an in-patient treatment facility. Its main hall boasts an irregular circular design with a flooring pattern made up of alternating red and white tiles, and walls painted in light blue and white.

To the right of the hall, one can find the Ultrasound Room B and the Ophthalmology Outpatient Department, while the corridor on the left leads to other medical departments. A centrally located staircase grants access to the second floor, housing the Traditional Chinese Medicine consultation rooms and the in-patient infusion area. The primary role of this health center is to provide regular medical and healthcare services to the residents of the Daquan Tatar People Township.

卫生院内 *Within the township hospital*

赛马 *Horse race*

（三）体育 Sports

新疆 塔塔尔族传统体育项目中很多是由生产劳动的一些场景逐渐演变而来的，通过与其他民族文化的交往交流交融，体育项目变得更加丰富多彩，如农闲时节会举行摔跤、爬杆、套麻袋跑等比赛，以娱乐为目的。塔塔尔族是一个以骑马闻名的民族，在撒班节会举行赛走马、赛奔马等比赛，充分体现了塔塔尔族群众爱好体育运动的特点。

赛马 *Horse race*

27

In Xinjiang, many of the Tatar people's traditional sports have roots in various labor and production activities. Over time, and through interaction, exchange, and integration with other cultures, these sports have diversified. For instance, during agricultural downtime, events like wrestling, pole climbing, and hemp hug running are held for recreational purposes. The Tatar people, known for their proficiency in horse riding, also commemorate the Saban Festival. During this celebration, they organize various competitions that highlight their sporting inclinations, such as horse walking races, sprinting horse races.

摔跤 *Wrestling*

塔塔尔族 其先民最初信仰原始宗教，后来相继信仰祆教、摩尼教、景教等。当伊斯兰教传入后，其宗教信仰转变为以伊斯兰教为主，多种宗教信仰并存，还有一些塔塔尔人不信仰宗教。

Historically, the Tatar ancestors were rooted in primitive religions, later transitioning through Zoroastrianism, Manichaeism, and Nestorianism. However, with the introduction of Islam, a major shift occurred in their religious orientation, leading many to embrace Islam as their primary faith. This resulted in a diverse religious tapestry among the Tatar people, with some practicing multiple religions, while others are non-religious or follow different faiths.

塔塔尔族 禁止在水池、水井、涝坝附近洗衣服和在坝内洗澡、游泳；忌讳在室内大小便；忌与子女开玩笑；不准在住房附近、墓地周围大小便，倒脏水。塔塔尔族人十分注意环境的保护，倡导人与自然协调发展。

Their cultural taboos and conventions are reflective of a deep respect for their environment and surroundings. For instance, they strictly refrain from washing clothes near water bodies such as pools, wells, or dams. Bathing or swimming inside a dam is also prohibited. Inside their homes, there's a strong aversion to using the indoor spaces for relieving oneself. On a social note, jesting with one's children is frowned upon. Furthermore, it's deemed inappropriate to relieve oneself or discard dirty water in the vicinity of homes or graveyards. These conventions underline the Tatar community's pronounced commitment to environmental protection and their advocacy for a harmonious relationship between mankind and nature.

冬牧场 *Winter pasture*

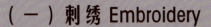

（一）刺绣 Embroidery

塔塔尔族的 妇女爱好刺绣，她们绣出的绣品色彩艳丽、针法清晰、层次分明，以精巧传神著称。塔塔尔族主要在帽子、坎肩、披肩、腰带、壶套、连衣裙等用品上刺绣各种花卉图案。

艺术
Art

正在刺绣的塔塔尔族妇女
Tatar women embroidering

坐垫 *Cushion*

花毯 *Dimity*

Women of the Tatar tribe are passionate about embroidery, creating pieces known for their vibrant colors, clear stitch work, and distinct layering. These intricacies give their embroideries a well-deserved reputation. The Tatar primarily adorn items such as hats, waistcoats, shawls, belts, kettle covers, and dresses with intricate floral designs.

圆顶花帽 *Domed flower hat*

尖顶帽 *Cap with a visor*

在 生活习俗的影响下，新疆塔塔尔族刺绣纹饰有写实性和抽象性的植物纹样。在图案的组合上，多采用方格纹、树纹和菱格纹等几何纹样，刺绣图案不论写实、写意都以植物枝叶、花卉多子果实为素材，画面布局富有韵律感。刺绣图案主要为植物枝蔓缠绕的卷草纹样等线性纹样与周边几何纹线条的结合；刺绣品的外沿衔接有蓬松的流苏，给人以动静结合的美感。

方巾和花毯
Square scarves and flower blankets

Influenced by their daily customs, the Tatar embroidery in Xinjiang features both realistic and abstract plant motifs. Their designs often incorporate geometric patterns like squares, tree motifs, and diamonds. The embroideries typically draw inspiration from plant stems, leaves, flowers, and fruits, presenting them in layouts that exude a rhythmic flow. The main designs showcase plant vines and other linear patterns intertwined with geometric outlines. The edges of these embroidered pieces are frequently adorned with fluffy tassels, offering a beautiful balance of motion and stillness.

（二）音乐 Music

塔塔尔族的 民歌优美动听，歌曲《天鹅进行曲》《白河边》等，尤为各民族群众青睐，传唱经久不衰。塔塔尔族民间音乐主要受到中国传统音乐体系的影响，同时也受到哈萨克族民间音乐自然小调与和声小调的影响。

The Tatar folk songs are melodious and heartwarming. Tunes such as the "Swan March" and "Beside the White River" remain evergreen, cherished by multiple ethnic groups. The musical heritage of the Tatar is deeply rooted in the traditional Chinese music system but also borrows elements from the natural and harmonic scales of Kazakh folk music.

男女对唱
Male and female duet

塔塔尔族 民间乐器有手风琴、七弦琴、库涅依、科比斯等。奇台县大泉乡的塔塔尔村民喜欢使用手风琴和冬不拉。手风琴是一种既能独奏，又能伴奏的键盘乐器，不仅能够演奏单声部的优美旋律，还可以演奏多声部的乐曲，更可以如钢琴一样双手演奏丰富的和声。冬不拉弹唱是塔塔尔族人民最喜爱的艺术表演形式，演唱者既可用于自弹自唱，也可用于独奏或乐器合奏，表现力非常丰富。而且它轻便，易于携带，可随时演奏，故深受人们的喜爱。

歌舞表演 Cabaret

Among the instruments favored by the Tatar are the accordion, the hepta-chord, kunieyi, and kebisi. In Daquan Village of Qitai County, Tatars often play the accordion and the dombra. The accordion, a versatile keyboard instrument, is adept at both solo and accompaniment roles. It can render melodies in singu-lar or multiple parts, allowing for the creation of intricate harmonies much like a piano. Dombra performances, often combined with singing, are particularly loved by the Tatar community. This instrument is expressive, compact, and portable, making it an ideal choice for spontaneous performances, and thus, holds a spe-cial place in their hearts.

乐器弹奏
Instrumental performance

（三）舞蹈 Dance

　　塔塔尔族 舞蹈动作灵巧、活泼，观赏性极强。塔塔尔族舞蹈还具有广泛的群众性，在节日喜庆时人们还会举行舞蹈比赛。例如，每到撒班节等节日时，只要听到手风琴的伴奏声，塔塔尔族人即会情不自禁地唱跳起来。其中青年人喜欢急速跳错步、开合步、蹲踢步、矮子步等；老年人喜用错步、错踮步、挥巾步等。舞蹈可男女对舞，亦可集体围成圆圈而跳，风格活泼。

舞蹈
Dance

塔塔尔族舞蹈表演
Tatar people dance performance

The dances of the Tatar people are characterized by their agile and lively movements, making them exceptionally captivating to watch. Moreover, Tatar dances enjoy widespread participation among the community, with dance competitions often held during festive occasions. For instance, during festivals like the Saban Festival, upon hearing the accompaniment of an accordion, the Tatar people are instinctively moved to sing and

塔塔尔族舞蹈表演
Tatar people dance performance

dance. Young Tatars particularly enjoy dance moves like rapid missteps, open-close steps, squat-kick steps, and "dwarf steps." In contrast, the older generation prefers moves such as missteps, incorrect tiptoe steps, and towel-waving steps. The dance can be performed in pairs, with a male and female counterpart, or collectively in a circle, radiating a vibrant and spirited style.

男女合舞
Co dance

舞蹈表演 *Dance performance*

（一）服饰 Clothing

衣食住
Food, Clothing, and Shelter

塔塔尔族小伙服饰
Tatar boy clothing

塔塔尔族 男性上身喜欢穿宽袖直领、对襟开胸、领边和袖口上绣有"十"字花纹或花草纹样的白衬衫，外加黑色齐腰的坎肩，或者是黑长衫，腰扎皮带。裤子一般是黑色，宽裆紧腿。夏天他们喜欢戴黑色、黑白两色或绿、橙、紫红色的丝绒绣花小帽，冬天则戴黑色卷毛皮帽。塔塔尔族女性喜欢穿紧腿裤和宽大的下边带皱边的连衫长裙子，上装袖口较小，颜色多为白、黄、绛色。脚上多穿皮鞋。她们还喜欢戴

服饰 *Clothing*

镶有珍珠的丝绒小花帽，少妇和年长的妇女还要在小帽上披丝头巾，或用
耳环、手镯、戒指、项链、胸针等物品装扮自己。有时她们还用质地细腻、
柔软舒适的绸缎或羊呢料剪裁成连衣褶裙，上身再搭配金丝绒披肩，看上
去风姿绰约，美丽动人。

服饰
Clothing

Tatar men prefer white shirts with wide sleeves and straight collars, characterized by embroideries of cross patterns or floral designs on the collar and cuffs. Over these shirts, they wear black waistcoats that reach the waist or full-length black robes, and these are often cinched at the waist with belts. Their trousers are typically black, featuring a broad crotch but tight-fitting legs. In the summer, they favor velvet turbans in shades such as black, black and white, green, orange, or burgundy. Come winter, they switch to black curly fur hats. Tatar women tend to wear leggings paired with wide, frill-edged floor-length dresses. Their tops, which feature smaller cuffs, mainly come in white, yellow, or crimson hues. They often sport leather shoes on their feet. They also have a penchant for small velvet hats adorned with pearls. Younger and older women alike often complement these hats with silk scarves and embellish themselves with accessories like earrings, bracelets, rings, necklaces, and brooches. At times, they might fashion dresses out of exquisite, soft silk or wool, paired with golden velvet shawls, presenting an elegant and captivating appearance.

塔塔尔族早餐 *Tatar breakfast*

　　塔塔尔族的 饮食文化多姿多彩，常用食材有牛、羊、鸡、鸭、鱼，还有鸡蛋、牛奶、面粉等。塔塔尔族主食习惯吃用肉、面、大米、土豆做的"卡特卡特"，还有"烤面饼"、抓饭、拌面、馕等。他们食用的蔬菜主要有土豆、南瓜、番茄、白菜、洋葱、胡萝卜等。最富有特色的风味食品是"古巴地亚"和"卡巴克阿什"。"古巴地亚"是将大米洗净后晾干，覆奶油、杏干、葡萄干，再放在火炉中烤制而成的一种饼，其味香甜可口。"卡巴克阿什"做法与"古巴地亚"相同，只不过盛饭容器是南瓜，再加人米和肉。

The Tatar culinary culture is diverse and colorful. Their diet often comprises beef, mutton, chicken, duck, fish, eggs, milk, and flour. A common staple in Tatar cuisine is "kate kate", a dish made from meat, noodles, rice, and potatoes. They also relish dishes like baked pastries, pilaf, noodles mixed with a sauce, and naan. Vegetables frequently consumed include potatoes, pumpkins, tomatoes, cabbage, onions, and carrots. Two uniquely Tatar dishes stand out: göbädiä and kabakeashi. Göbädiä is a delicacy where clean, dried rice is layered with cream, dried apricots, and raisins, then baked to perfection, resulting in a delightfully sweet taste. Kabakeashi, on the other hand, is similarly prepared but uses a pumpkin shell as a container, adding rice and meat to the mix. Tatar women excel in crafting a variety of pastries, notable not just for their taste but also for their aesthetic appeal. While they are aficionados of different tea varieties, they also have a taste for horse and camel milk. Locally, two beverages – quas and kesaile – are particularly popular. Quas is akin to beer, brewed from the fermentation of honey and hops, while kesaile is a wine made from wild grapes.

塔塔尔族早餐 *Tatar breakfast*

塔塔尔族 妇女善于制作各种糕点，她们做出来的糕点，不仅味美可口、品种繁多，而且形状也很美观。塔塔尔族除喜欢饮用各类茶以外，还喜欢喝马奶和驼奶。受到当地人普遍喜爱的饮料是"卡瓦斯"和"克赛勒"。卡瓦斯类似啤酒，是用蜂蜜和啤酒花发酵后酿制而成的；克赛勒是用野葡萄酿制而成的酒。

糕点，Cake

49

In terms of beverages, the Tatar people enjoy various types of tea, as well as horse milk and camel milk. The drinks favored by the local population are *quas* and *kesaile*. *Quas* is produced through the fermentation of honey and hops, resembling the production method of beer, whereas *kesaile* is a type of alcohol crafted using wild grapes.

馓子 *Sanzi*

酸奶疙瘩 *Yogurt lumps*

婚礼餐前小食 Wedding pre-dinner snacks

特色美食

　　塔塔尔族⋯⋯餐，早晚多用⋯⋯午吃正餐。日常以面、肉、奶为主体，也吃大米、蔬菜和水果。塔塔尔族妇女心
高超，善⋯⋯饼和糕点而闻⋯⋯
　　塔塔尔⋯⋯兰教。禁忌与其⋯⋯伊斯兰教的民族一样。主要节日除肉孜节和古尔邦节外，还有撒班节。
　　在饮食⋯⋯以烹调著称的塔塔⋯⋯于制作各种糕点，用鸡蛋和面粉制成的小馕以精制可口而驰名。节日和待客
了抓饭，还⋯⋯⋯⋯焙的两种糕点"古拜地埃"和"伊特白里可"是塔塔尔族特有的风味食
有类⋯⋯⋯⋯大米和⋯⋯⋯⋯用野葡萄制成的"克赛勒"酒。
　　⋯⋯⋯⋯干⋯⋯⋯⋯⋯⋯"）、面条、抓饭、馅饼、各种烤馕等。另外，还喜欢喝牛奶、羊奶、
⋯⋯⋯柿、黄萝卜等蔬菜作为菜肴。

塔塔尔族美食展示 Exhibition of Tatar people cuisine

（三）民居 Shelter

塔塔尔族 在农牧区的房屋多用土坯、砖块、木材、石块等材料建筑，有土房、木房之分。房顶为"人"字形，上盖铁皮，刷绿色或其他颜色的油漆；也建平顶屋，上有很厚的草泥。平顶房房屋从整体结构上看，呈长方体，在屋顶饰以多层次的黄色砖或青色砖，在墙基上亦砌上明显的有色砖进行装饰，给单调的房屋镶上优美的轮廓线。民居的窗户上也饰有图案，有的呈"山"字形，状如皇冠，清新自然。

民居模型
Residential model

民居 *Residential houses*

In the agricultural and pastoral areas, the Tatar community predominantly constructs their homes using materials like mudbrick, brick, timber, and stone. These dwellings are distinguished as either earth houses or log houses. A common roofing style is the herringbone pattern, overlaid with iron sheets that are often painted green or other colors. There's also a prevalent flat-roof design, which is substantially layered with grass and mud for insulation. Architecturally, these residences usually showcase a rectangular form, with flat roofs highlighted by multiple tiers of either yellow or blue bricks. Additionally, the foundation walls are embellished with vividly colored bricks, introducing an elegant outline to the otherwise simplistic houses. The house windows are often accented with intricate designs, some resembling the Chinese character for "mountain" or shapes reminiscent of crowns, exuding a touch of regality and freshness.

塔塔尔族 民居多是套间，房外一般都建有围墙，自成院落。院内种植树木、花草，修有小道、走廊，建有厕所、棚圈、菜窖等。

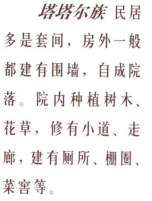

民居内部 *Inside residential houses*

窗檐造型 *Window eaves design*

Most Tatar residences adopt a suite-like design, encompassed by exterior walls that lead into individual courtyards. These enclosed spaces are brought to life with trees, flowering plants, and grasses. Within these courtyards, residents lay out walkways, corridors, and often establish amenities like toilets, shelters, and vegetable storage pits.

民居内部 *Inside residential houses*

（一）婚礼 Wedding Ceremony

奇台县 大泉塔塔尔族乡的青年结婚时，一般在宴会厅举行典礼。新郎新娘和他们的朋友一起，从婚车上下来，在手风琴演奏者欢快的音乐声中进入宴会厅。此时，宴会厅门口已经站好了迎接的队伍。宴会厅里面还坐着新人家中德高望重的亲属。新人面向他们行礼问好，并友好地拥抱。伴随着司仪播放的乐曲，婚礼正式开始。一位新娘的女性长辈向台上的新人及其重要亲属抛撒糖果，寓意将幸福与喜悦传递给更多的人。新人聆听长辈教诲之后共饮一杯蜂蜜水，象征婚后生活如蜜般甜蜜。婚礼结束，娱乐活动开始。音乐响起，宾客们纷纷走进舞池跳舞，整个宴会厅充满幸福和喜悦的氛围。

婚礼仪式 *Wedding Ceremony*

塔塔尔族婚礼撒糖环节
Sugar sprinkling at Tatar wedding

In the Daquan Tatar People Township of Qitai County, Tatar wedding ceremonies are commonly conducted in a banquet hall. As the bride, groom, and their friends alight from their wedding vehicles, they walk into the hall to the cheerful notes of an accordionist playing. At the entrance, a welcoming group awaits them, and inside the hall are esteemed relatives from both families. The newlyweds greet these relatives with salutations and embrace them warmly. With the start of ceremonial music, the wedding proceedings commence. An elder female from the bride's side takes the stage to sprinkle candies over the newlyweds and significant family members, symbolizing the dissemination of happiness and joy. After heeding advice from the elders, the couple shares a drink of honey water, illustrating the promise of a sweet marital life ahead. The official ceremony comes to an end, marking the beginning of festivities. As music fills the hall, guests take to the dance floor, creating an ambiance of pure happiness and joy.

婚礼迎宾 *Wedding welcome*　　　　　　婚礼答礼 *Wedding gift*

婚礼前表演 Pre-wedding performance

婚礼前舞蹈 Pre-wedding dance

　　婚后，新郎和新娘都要在女方家住一段时间，一般三个月或半年，有的甚至要生过一个孩子以后才回到男方家。塔塔尔族对待女婿如同对待亲生儿子一样。传统的塔塔尔族家庭是以一对夫妻和其子女组成的核心家庭为主，伴有一些两代夫妻的混合家庭。三四代人共同生活在一起的大家庭很少见。

Post-wedding, it's customary for the groom and bride to reside in the bride's home for a duration ranging between three to six months. Some couples might stay until after the birth of their first child before relocating to the groom's house. The Tatars treat sons-in-law just like their own sons.

新人入场
The newlyweds enter the venue

The typical Tatar family structure predominantly consists of a nuclear unit, though some families do include multiple generations. However, extensive multi-generational families are a rare sight among the Tatars.

新娘、新郎 *Bride and groom*

新郎家人致辞 *Speech by the groom's family*

男性宾客分食羊肉 *Male guests share lamb*

61

传统婚礼 *Traditional wedding*

撒班节宣传栏 *Satan billboard*

（二）撒班节 Saban Festival

　　塔塔尔族 主要节日有肉孜节（开斋节）、古尔邦节（宰牲节）、"纳鲁吾孜节"（春分）和"撒班节"（犁头节）。也过春节、端午节、中秋节等节日。

　　撒班节 是塔塔尔族特有的民族节日，亦称犁头节。"撒班"是用来犁地的新农具，它的产生结束了用十字镐翻地的岁月。因此，撒班节是塔塔尔族的祖先为纪念先进农具撒班的发明而确立的。

村公园步道 *Village park trail*

Among the principal festivals celebrated by the Tatar people are the Ruzi Festival (Eid al-Fitr), Corban Festival (Eid al-Adha), Nowruz Festival (Spring Equinox), and the Saban Festival (Plowshare Festival). They also partake in other Chinese festivals like the Spring Festival, Dragon Boat Festival, and the Mid-Autumn Festival.

铿锵奋进的脚步

续写春天的故事

庆祝中国共产党成立100周年
The 100th Anniversary of the Founding of
The Communist Party of China

实施乡村振兴战略
建设新时代美丽新农村

福州援疆
FUZHOU AID FOR XINJIANG

奇台县2022年
塔塔尔族撒班节

套麻袋跑 *Hemp bag running*

塔塔尔族 在每年春耕农忙结束后，会选择一个风景优美的地方举办撒班节。女子穿戴本民族服饰，男子则穿西装西裤，头戴小花帽，各个脸上洋溢着幸福的笑容。他们载歌载舞，相互祝贺，各种文艺汇演及体育项目相继上演。塔塔尔族传统体育竞技活动有"咬匙跑"比赛、摔跤、拔河、套麻袋跑等，其中"咬匙跑"最为风趣，也最受人们喜爱，参赛者口衔一匙，匙内放一只鸡蛋迅速向前跑，途中鸡蛋不能落地，最先到达目的地者为胜利。

咬匙跑 *Scoop snatching race*

The Saban Festival, also known as the Plowshare Festival, holds unique significance for the Tatar community. This festivity commemorates the advent of the 'saban', an innovative plowing tool that heralded the end of using pickaxes for tilling. Annually, upon concluding their spring plowing, the Tatars pick a scenic venue to hold the Saban Festival. Women grace the occasion in traditional attire, whereas men don Western suits paired with

撒班节开幕 *Opening of Sabbath*

男女对唱 *Male and female duet*

characteristic small floral caps. Everywhere, faces beam
with joy. The festival resonates with songs and dances, mu-
tual congratulations, and an array of cultural and athletic
performances. Traditional Tatar sports include the intriguing
egg snatching race , wrestling, tug-of-war, sack races,and
the amusing egg-and-spoon race where participants,holding
the spoon in their mouths, race without letting the egg fall.
The quickest runner who manages to keep the egg intact
wins.

撒班节篝火 *Saipan bonfire*

摔跤 Wrestling

71

夜幕降临，撒班节篝火晚会正式开始。伴随着节奏欢快的歌曲，人们围绕篝火转圈舞蹈，时而合着音乐节拍踢踏，时而抬手靠近篝火又迅速散开。有的人大声歌唱，有的人吹口哨助兴，总之，快乐的氛围充盈着整个现场。

撒班节合照 *Group photo of Sabbath*

As dusk approaches, the festival's bonfire gathering ignites. With lively tunes in the backdrop, attendees dance around the fire, occasionally moving rhythmically closer and then swiftly retreating. While some choose to express their happiness through song, others whistle to boost the festive spirit. Overall, the joyous ambiance is palpable throughout.

后记
Afterword

本书是在兰州大学西北少数民族研究中心的资助下完成的，在此，我要感谢赵利生主任的大力支持，感谢杨林坤处长为本书提供的大量有益的参考资料，还要感谢王建新教授无私的帮助。在田野调查阶段，奇台县大泉塔塔尔族乡党委领导、同志们的热情招待和知识上的指导，是我能够顺利完成图片拍摄和文字撰写的重要保障。大泉乡塔塔尔村民对我这个"陌生的朋友"给予了足够的耐心与温情。当我表明来意后，他们随即邀请我参加一年一度的撒班节和一场婚礼，对于这些朋友的慷慨相助，我难以用言辞表达感激之情。最后，感谢为本书顺利出版解决一系列问题的编辑老师。

赵璇　杨林坤
2023 年 9 月 12 日

This work was made possible with the generous support of the Center for Studies of Ethnic Minorities in Northwest China at Lanzhou University. I extend my heartfelt gratitude to Director Zhao Lisheng for his steadfast support, to Director Yang Linkun for offering invaluable reference materials, and to Professor Wang Jianxin for his selfless assistance. During the field research phase, the hospitality and guidance from the leadership and colleagues of the Party Committee in Daquan Tatar People Township, Qitai County, were instrumental in ensuring the seamless completion of both the photography and writing for this book. The Tatar villagers of Daquan Township embraced me, a "stranger," with incredible warmth and patience. Upon expressing my intentions, they graciously invited me to their annual Saban Festival and a wedding ceremony. My heartfelt gratitude for their kindness is beyond words. Lastly, my sincere thanks to the editorial team who tackled numerous challenges, paving the way for the smooth publication of this book.